That Dreamer:

Designing a Life You Love — Even Though, In Spite Of, and Just Because

By Elissa Stacy

"It's not a tragedy. it's a masterpiece."

This book is intended to inspire, motivate and initiate reflective thoughts for the reader. While the content of this book inspired the author to improve her personal wellbeing, your personal improvement will still require your hard work and determination. There is no magic formula for success.

The publisher does not have any control over and does not assume any responsibility for author or third-party websites or their content.

Cover art and design by Elissa Stacy

All Bible verses are from The ESV Study Bible: English Standard Version; Crossway Bibles: Wheaton, Ill, 2008.

Digital Design by Elissa Stacy

Publishing Services by Telemachus Press, LLC
7652 Sawmill Road, Suite 304
Dublin, Ohio 43016

Visit the author website: www.stacycodesigns.com

ISBN: 978-1-965121-36-8 (eBook)
ISBN: 978-1-965121-37-5 (Paperback)

Version 2025.09.28

Table of Contents

That Dreamer:

Designing a Life You Love — Even Though, In Spite Of, and Just Because

"

"YOU DONT KNOW THE VALUE OF A DREAM, UNTIL A DREAM IS ALL YOU HAVE"

ELISSA

Introduction: To the One Who's Still Dreaming

If I could sit across from you, heart to heart, this is what I'd say: You are not too broken. You are not too far gone. It is never too late to dream again.

I've always had a story to tell. For as long as I can remember, I was that dreamer, the one who believed there had to be more, even when life said otherwise. I held on to hope like it was oxygen. Sometimes it was all I had.

I've walked through things I didn't think I'd survive. Abuse. Heartbreak. Darkness. I've wrestled with shame, silence, and the weight of trying to be everything for everyone while feeling like I was falling apart inside. But somehow, some way, I kept going. I kept dreaming.

This book is the story of how I designed a life I love, even though it was hard, in spite of what happened to me, and just because I knew I was made for more.

It's about healing. It's about faith. It's about choosing joy and purpose on the other side of pain. And most of all, it's about daring to dream when the world tells you to settle.

Whether you're in the thick of your struggle or standing at the edge of your breakthrough, I want you to know: you are not alone.

If you've ever questioned your worth... If you've ever had to rebuild from the ground up... If you've ever dared to dream in the dark...

This book is for you.

So take a breath. Take my hand. And let's walk this journey together, from broken to bold, from barely surviving to fully alive.

This is my story. But it might just help you find yours.

You are that dreamer. And you're just getting started.

66

"HE HAS MADE EVERYTHING BEAUTIFUL IN ITS TIME."

ECCLESIASTES 3:11

Chapter 1: The Girl with the Dream

"Here comes THAT Dreamer"

Before I ever knew pain, I knew possibility.

I was just a little girl, wide-eyed, curious, and full of wonder. Life around me might have been messy, uncertain, or even painful, but inside me lived something different: a dream. It didn't have a name or a clear picture back then, but it pulsed quietly in my heart like a whisper I couldn't ignore.

I dreamed of safety. Of joy. Of a home filled with laughter, not tension. I dreamed of being seen, known, loved for who I was, not what I could endure. I didn't want to just survive, I wanted to live. Really live.

Maybe I didn't have the words for it yet, but deep down, I believed there was more than what I was born into. More than dysfunction. More than silence. More than shame. There was this something in me that said, You were created for more.

I escaped in daydreams, imagining a future where I was free, strong, and smiling. I didn't know how to get there, but somehow, dreaming helped me breathe through the hard days.

That little girl, that dreamer, was the beginning of everything.

She didn't know her voice would one day rise from the ashes. She didn't know she'd grow up to be a mother, a creator, a builder of safe spaces. She didn't know that her story would matter, not just to her, but to others too.

But still, she dreamed.

Even though I was raised in chaos and born into pain... Even though I carried trauma before I even knew what that word meant... Even though I cried myself to sleep more nights than not, prayed for a different life, and sometimes wished it would all just stop.

Even though, I survived.

And not just survived, I made a vow. I would build a different life. I would learn how to love, how to heal, how to dream, even if no one ever showed me how.

The journey to designing a life you love doesn't begin when everything is perfect. It begins when life is at its messiest. For me, it began as a little girl, standing alone in a world that didn't seem to have room for her. A girl who looked around and saw brokenness but somehow held onto something unbreakable inside: hope.

When I was in third grade, I had already lived through more than many kids my age should ever have to endure. But one moment stands out to me, like a flash of light in the darkness.

I was out front raking leaves. It was just another ordinary day in what often felt like a heavy life. And then, suddenly, a black van pulled up to the curb. People in suits jumped out, holding a two-liter bottle of soda like they were delivering something precious.

I stood there stunned, filled with something I hadn't felt before.

Joy.

It was so sudden, so full, that I didn't even know how to contain it. My heart leapt, and for a moment, I thought, We've won the lottery. I thought they were there for us. For me.

Turns out, they were just Kirby vacuum salesmen.

But it didn't matter.

Because in that moment, I felt something awaken in me that I had never felt before: a sense of joy... and freedom.

It was the first time I remember feeling like life could surprise me with something good.

That feeling never left me.

Even as life continued to throw its weight on my shoulders, I longed for that freedom. To live life on my own terms. To breathe without fear. To be one of those people who wasn't just surviving life but actually living it.

For a long time, I thought there were only two kinds of people in the world: those who made life go 'round and those who were actually living it.

I wanted to live.

By sixth grade, life still felt heavy. My mom worked nights, and that morning she wasn't home yet. My oldest brother had to drive me to school, and it was the kind of drive that made my skin crawl, rowdy, reckless, loud. My wet hair clung to my head, and I remember feeling so small, so unseen, so wrong.

I hated myself that day.

But when I got to school, something unexpected happened. We had a substitute teacher. She wheeled in one of those old TVs on the tall metal cart. "We're going to watch a TED Talk," she said.

Then she looked right at me.

"Your hair is beautiful," she said.

It stopped me in my tracks. I don't think anyone had ever said something like that to me before, especially when I felt so low.

It was like she tuned right into the part of me that needed to be seen.

That day, I didn't just hear her words, I believed them. Something flickered inside me as I watched that TED Talk. A light turned on. A fire ignited.

Right then, I said to myself:

"I'm going to do that. I'm going to share my story. I'm going to help people. I'm going to be an author. A speaker. Someone who brings hope."

That moment became my anchor.

Through every storm, every setback, every heartache... I held on to that dream. It became the light that kept me going, even in my darkest nights.

Because deep down, I always knew:

I was that dreamer.

If I could say anything to that little girl, the one raking leaves, the one who flinched at chaos, the one who sat wide-eyed watching a TED Talk with a spark in her chest, I'd whisper this:

Just keep going. Don't look back. The pain doesn't define you.

The chaos isn't your future. The way they see you isn't the truth of who you are.

Have peace, sweet girl. Have patience. You're going to make it.

And not just make it, you're going to rise. You're going to heal. You're going to love your life. It will be better than you ever dreamed, even in your wildest hopes.

You are not forgotten. You are not invisible. You are becoming.

You are that dreamer.

"He has made everything beautiful in its time."

— Ecclesiastes 3:11

Chapter Reflection:

1.The Girl with the Dream

What dreams did you carry as a child that still whisper to your heart today? Have you silenced them or are they still speaking?

Let's Pray Together:

God, help me remember the dreams You placed in my heart before the world told me to shrink. Remind me of who I was before I learned to doubt myself. Awaken wonder in me again, and give me the courage to believe that I was made for more.

"

"IT'S NOT A TRAGEDY. IT'S A MASTERPIECE."

Chapter 2: The Turning Point—When the Dream Began to Pull Through

"The weight I carried"

There wasn't just one turning point in my story, there were many. Like waves, each one came a little stronger, crashing against the shore of who I was and shaping who I was becoming.

One of the first came when my oldest son was just three years old. He stood in front of me, so small, so pure, and I remember looking into his eyes and thinking, He deserves more. I didn't know exactly what that "more" looked like, but I knew I wanted to give it to him. I didn't want him to grow up in chaos, confusion, or pain. And in that moment, I realized something else: I didn't want to either.

That moment was quiet but it stirred something deep in me. It was the first time I truly saw myself as a mother who could fight for her children and for herself. It planted a seed of strength I didn't know I had.

Not long after, I ran into the man who would become my husband, the boy I met in high school who I thought was too good for me. Like, I had too many broken pieces, the one who would later adopt my children and prove that love doesn't always leave. I grew up without a father. I had stepdads who never really cared about me. I didn't know what it meant to be safe in the presence of a man. But this man was different. He didn't just love me, he loved them. They chose him, and he chose them. He claimed them as his own.

It showed me that life could look different. That maybe I wasn't doomed to repeat the past.

Still, healing doesn't happen all at once. Even as our family grew, I was still battling the trauma that lived inside me. When I had our fourth child, something in me shifted again. The weight of everything I had survived felt heavier than ever but this time, I didn't push it down. I couldn't. I knew something had to change.

I remember sitting with God in complete desperation. I told Him, "If

You heal me, I will never again silence my story. When You nudge me to speak, I will. When You lead me to write, I will. Even if no one is listening, I will keep going."

That moment marked the beginning of my healing. I was clinging to the hem of His garment, begging for breakthrough.

I began stepping into what I now call my FitWithin journey, not just physical wellness, but emotional and spiritual alignment. I started confronting my pain. I looked at my beliefs. I tried to understand why I felt what I felt, why I reacted the way I did. It was like waking up after years of sleepwalking.

And it was then, when I was most raw, most open, that I told my husband how I truly felt.

"My life feels like a tragedy," I said, through tears.

He didn't flinch. He didn't offer a cliché. He looked me straight in the eye and said, "No. It's a masterpiece."

Something cracked open in me.

It was like God Himself used those words to echo a truth I hadn't yet been able to claim. And I believed him. Because I believed in his walk with God. I believed in the way he saw me. I knew his story, but he also knew mine. And that made all the difference.

That was the real turning point, not just the moment I wanted more, but the moment I believed I could have it. That my story didn't have to end in survival. That maybe, just maybe, it could lead to joy.

I often say that in the early days, I was just dipping my toes into healing. But after that moment, I was walking straight into the water, with no looking back. I didn't know what would unravel next, but I was finally willing to see.

And that's when everything began to change.

"It's not a tragedy. It's a masterpiece."

Chapter Reflection:

2. The Turning Point—When the Dream Began to Pull Through

Can you identify a moment in your life when everything began to shift? What was God revealing to you about yourself in that season?

Let's Pray Together:

Lord, thank You for the moments that shift everything. Even when I didn't understand the pain, You were pulling me forward. Help me to see Your hand in the turning points of my story, and give me peace in the process.

"

"NOW FAITH IS
THE SUBSTANCE
OF THINGS
HOPED FOR, THE
EVIDENCE OF
THE UNSEEN."

HEBREWS 11:1

Chapter 3: In Spite Of—Becoming Who I Was Always Meant to Be

"I wanted more"

In spite of the pain, the poverty, the trauma, and the statistics stacked against me...

In spite of being told I was "too much" or "not enough"...

In spite of being overlooked, underestimated, and undervalued...

I became,

Not all at once, and not without breaking, but I became.

For years, I was surviving. But somewhere along the way, I started to heal. Healing wasn't a one-time event, it was a thousand small choices. Choosing to keep showing up. Choosing to believe there was more. Choosing to see myself not as damaged, but as designed, on purpose, with purpose.

Motherhood didn't fix me, but it revealed me.

It showed me every wound I had buried, every lie I had believed, and every ounce of strength I didn't know I had. It wasn't the end of my dreams, it was the beginning of my becoming. The fire that refined me.

I started to create. To dream again. To believe that I was worthy of building something beautiful, not because I had it all figured out, but because I was willing to try.

And that's where entrepreneurship came in.

I didn't have a business plan. I didn't even have a business background. What I had was vision and a fierce determination to design a life that felt aligned, not just successful by the world's standards, but fulfilling by my own.

So I started messy. I started scared.

I built FitWithin from the inside out because the truth is, transformation doesn't start in the gym. It starts in your mind. In your spirit. In your decision to become more than what you've been through.

Then I launched Tees for Truth, a mission to clothe others not just in fabric, but in truth. For every shirt sold, one is donated to someone in need. I wanted people to wear something that meant something.

Because I know what it's like to have nothing. I know what it's like to want to give your kids the world and have no idea how you'll pay for groceries. I've been on both sides, the one in need and the one called to meet a need.

And I wanted to be the kind of woman who does both, who gives even when she's still healing, who shows up even when she's unsure, who leads with love even when life hasn't been kind.

Healing gave me a new lens. I started to see my story not as a burden, but as a bridge, a way to connect with others and say, "Me too. And if I can rise, so can you."

People often ask how I do it all, motherhood, business, marriage, homeschooling, healing. And the truth is, I don't "do it all."

But I do show up for what matters most.

I've learned to delegate what I can, release what I can't control, and trust that I was never meant to build alone. I've found mentors, friends, and faith to carry me when I couldn't carry myself.

In spite of it all, I kept going.

And now, I teach my children to dream. I speak life over them, I show them what it looks like to keep showing up, to build something out of brokenness, to fight for joy, to choose integrity, to lead with heart.

Because healing doesn't mean the past disappears.

It means it no longer defines you.

And if you let it—it can even refine you.

"Now faith is the substance of things hoped for, the evidence of the unseen."
—Hebrews 11:1

Chapter Reflection:

3. In Spite Of—Becoming Who I Was Always Meant to Be

What have you overcome that could've destroyed you but didn't? Who are you becoming because of that?

Let's Pray Together:

God, You saw me through every dark place I've walked. In spite of what I've been through, You are still writing beauty into my story. Help me shed shame and stand tall in who You say I am. Give me boldness to become all I was meant to be.

66

"HE THOUGHT
HE STOLE IT
FROM ME, NOW
IT'S BECOME MY
TESTIMONY."

Chapter 4: The Knock at the Door

"The Breaking Point"

The hardest door I ever had to walk through was the one that led to healing.

After my surgery, I began weaning myself off all the medications they told me I'd need forever. Pain pills. Anxiety meds. Antidepressants. One by one, I let them go. Slowly, painfully, I detoxed from all of it. I trembled. I cried. I felt like I was losing my mind.

But I also felt like I was giving myself a chance, maybe for the first time ever, to really live.

One day, I picked up my dad's Bible. The one he used in prison. Inside, written in his handwriting, were the words: "Enough is enough."

Somehow, I knew those words were for me.

That same day, I Googled something that shifted everything:

"What does trauma do to a child's brain?"

And what I found unlocked something inside of me. There it was in black and white, how trauma affects development, hijacks the nervous system, impacts behavior, memory, relationships... everything. I sat there reading, heart pounding, as I realized:

These weren't character flaws.

These were symptoms.

This was trauma.

And for the first time, I saw myself with compassion.

At thirty years old, it felt like the pillow had finally been lifted from my face. I could breathe.

I went to a brain doctor for a scan. He looked at my results and said gently, "Everything you've struggled with... it's all here. This is trauma brain. What others have labeled as anxiety or ADHD is actually your brain stuck in survival."

I needed deep treatment. About $6,000 worth. But I didn't have that kind of money.

So I got creative. I became a student of healing. I pressed into my "fitwithin" journey. I studied the nervous system. I read everything I could. I prayed. I journaled. I got still. I listened. And I leaned heavily on the only strength I could count on God's.

I was finally ready to speak the truth.

With my husband's support, I called the sheriff's department and said the words I'd never said aloud:

"I need to file a report."

A deputy came to my house. I wrote it all down. My hands trembled. My voice shook. I felt exposed and small.

They asked me to come in for a formal interview.

I went alone.

Halfway through, the detective paused and brought in a victim's advocate to sit with me. It was too much. I was unraveling.

"I know it's been a long time," I said. "But I had no one. No one would've believed me. No one did."

But this time, they did.

They believed me.

And in that moment, a door opened.

No matter what came next, I had finally spoken the truth. And that was the beginning of freedom.

Behind the scenes, I was still running with the PTA. Smiling at events. Cheering for my kids. Writing books. Still starting a business and a charity. Loving my family. The weight of years, the trauma, the pressure, the exhaustion, it caught up with my marriage too. My husband and I were strained, trying to hold everything together. No one knew what I was carrying. Not really.

But behind closed doors, I was in therapy, and I cried. The pain still lived in me, even as I was learning how to heal.

I told a group of women at Bible study once that I longed for a time in my life when I would feel secure in my relationship with the Lord, when I wouldn't have to cling to the hem of His garment just to make it through the day.

But that season wasn't that time.

After being so trapped in fear afraid to die, but also afraid to live,

I had to cling.

I had to shut out every voice that wasn't leading me toward healing.

I had to put on blinders and fix my eyes on Jesus.

Because that's how desperate I was.

Because that's how ready I was.

Because that's what healing costs, it costs everything that isn't real.

This was the knock at the door.

And I was finally brave enough to open it.

Facing the Past, Standing in Strength

Picture a woman being held by her hand, walking toward the very thing that had tormented her whole life. Children hide behind her back while tears stream down her face and blood runs from her nose. Her body is covered with bruises. She cries to the hand holding hers and says, "Please no. I'm scared. I don't know if I can do it!"

Her voice trembles as she pleads with the gentle hand. Still, they keep walking.

"I'll never fit in! Why does this have to be my story?" she cries, hunched over, face in her hands. "What a tragedy!"

Then, all at once, the tears dry. The nose is wiped clean. The bruises fade. And she stands tall, shoulders back, chin up. Her heart stops racing as a comforting voice and calmness settle over her.

She hears it clearly:

"Because Elissa, you weren't made to fit in. You were born to stand out. And your story isn't a tragedy at all. It's a masterpiece."

"He thought he stole it from me, now it's become my testimony."

Chapter Reflection:

4. The Knock at the Door

What unexpected moment challenged everything you thought you were ready for? Did you rise or retreat? What did you learn?

Let's Pray Together:

Father, when life comes crashing in, help me not to fear. Even when I feel unprepared, remind me You are already in the room. Help me open the door with faith, knowing You go before me. Let me trust You when the unexpected comes.

❝

"I'M WRITING MY OWN TREATMENT PLAN."

Chapter 5: More Than a Childhood

"The Work of Healing"

They say healing comes in layers, and they're right. I didn't wake up one day completely healed, whole, and free. No. It was messy. It was raw. And it took everything in me to keep going.

As someone who has struggled my entire life with depression and anxiety, it became necessary to my emotional, physical, and spiritual well-being to be as wholesome, true, and authentic to myself as I possibly could be. It's like a full-time job. If I'm not intentional, I tank.

I always say, "I may have anxiety, but it doesn't have me." But the truth is, it can have me. It has before. And that's why I'm constantly growing. Constantly peeling back the layers so I can keep moving forward and not stay stuck in the places that tried to destroy me.

As I started unpacking it all, I realized how much weight I was still carrying from childhood. And healing? It wasn't glamorous. It was more like raising a newborn. But that baby was me.

Just like you'd hold and nurture a baby through sleepless nights and endless cries, I had to hold myself. I had to re-parent myself. Give myself what I never received. That's the work of healing.

There were days filled with tears. Anger. Sadness. And confusion. Days I couldn't escape the pain, no matter how hard I tried. I felt like I was living in a glass bowl, watching the world go on while I stayed stuck, sliding back down every time I tried to climb out.

Children who experience trauma don't understand. They see life through a shattered lens, and they need to be met with love, patience, and understanding. But they can be healed. I'm living proof.

I've been surprised by my own strength, first as a single mother, then as a wife, and most of all, by the woman I've become today. But I've learned this: It's my weakness that makes me strong. Because that's where God's glory shows up. Because I am weak, He is strong.

I love allowing myself to be a woman, gentle, kind, tenderhearted, and it's all because of Jesus. The Bible says that children are like arrows in a warrior's quiver, and my children are my arrows. I always say I've been given a second chance at childhood by raising them.

I love being a mother. I love watching them grow. I haven't done it perfectly, and there were times I parented through my trauma without even realizing it. But therapy helped me see that. It taught me that I was doing the best I could with what I knew at the time. And now? I know better.

Childhood is so much more than a season of life. It's the foundation for how we see the world, people, relationships, and even how we dare to dream.

One day, my counselor told me not to devalue the fact that I've raised my children in an environment I never had. She said, "They don't know what you knew. They have a different life because you created it."

And she was right. I built this for them.

I built it with faith in what I could not yet see.

"Now faith is the substance of things hoped for, the evidence of things not seen." Hebrews 11:1

And it's etched into the fabric of my soul

"I'm writing my own treatment plan."

66

"SET YOUR OWN
THERMOSTAT."

— DEION SANDERS

Chapter Reflection:

5. More Than a Childhood

How has your childhood shaped the way you see yourself today? What are you working to unlearn or reframe?

Let's Pray Together:

God, I give You the parts of my story I didn't choose. Heal the child in me who needed more love, more safety, more joy. Teach me how to parent myself with gentleness and grace. Thank You for giving me the chance to break generational cycles.

Chapter 6: The Road Less Traveled

"Choosing to Dream Again"

There's a reason that phrase shows up in poems, books, and sermons.

Because once you step onto that road, the road less traveled, you don't come back the same.

For me, it began when I made the decision to stop running from myself and finally walk headfirst into healing. Not the kind of healing that feels good or looks pretty. I'm talking about gut-wrenching, soul-twisting, face-the-pain kind of healing. The kind that makes you want to turn around every five steps but you don't.

I remember reading The Road Less Traveled by M. Scott Peck. It cracked something open in me. For the first time, I didn't feel like a disaster. I felt seen. Understood. Like maybe, just maybe, there was meaning in the pain. Maybe my path wasn't broken, maybe it was just different.

That book gave language to the ache I carried. It taught me that discipline, love, and grace weren't signs of weakness, but tools for growth. That walking the harder road doesn't make you weak, it makes you brave.

And somewhere in the middle of the mess, I had a dream.

My papaw lifted me onto a shelf, like I was something valuable. Something treasured. When I woke up, I looked in the mirror and, for the first time, I saw someone beautiful.

Not because I was flawless. Not because everything had been fixed.

But because I was still standing.

Because even on the road less traveled, I hadn't given up.

This was the chapter where I started choosing different. Yes, I was healing, but I was also finally choosing me. My life. My peace. My joy. I began sprinkling in the fun, the beauty, and the freedom I'd always dreamed of. The freedom to make a living doing what I love.

To design my life from the inside out.

I began building the life I had longed for, the one where I could be the mom I always dreamed of being. Spending time with my children so I wouldn't one day look back and wish I had. Designing my home. My days. My identity.

Ultimately, this is where I began designing my life, so that both my little girl self and my older self would be proud.

And that has made all the difference.

"Set your own thermostat."
—Deion Sanders

Chapter Reflection:

6. The Road Less Traveled

What part of your healing journey feels the most lonely? What keeps you walking, even when the path is unclear?

Let's Pray Together:

Lord, this road is hard, but I know You walk it with me. Give me strength when I feel alone. Remind me why I started, and help me trust that every step is shaping me for something greater. Keep me steady when I feel like turning back.

"

**"I KNOW THE
RULES. NOW
TELL ME THE
FINE."**

— JOHN MAXWELL

Chapter 7: From Hell to Honey

"Designing a Life YOU Love"

This wasn't just about childhood trauma. It wasn't just a few bad years.

It was a lifetime of feeling unsafe in this world, like I was always on the run, always alone.

At 17, I moved out and never really stopped running. I found myself in circles I never imagined, caught up in drugs, arrested for things I barely remember doing. The weight of trauma doesn't just live in your past. It follows you into your future if you let it.

When I was 18, I got arrested again, this time as an adult. That changed everything. The fight that landed me there started with my brother, the same brother who beat me up on the playground in 3rd grade. This time, it ended with him wailing on me in my own room. My best friend, tired of seeing my pain, jumped in. The cops were called. I ended up in jail, 26 hours, sleeping on the floor in a potato sack. And the worst part? My family didn't bail me out.

I was sentenced to two years of mandatory anger management. I got kicked out twice. I had to stand in front of the judge, humbly ask for forgiveness, and plead to be let back in. People kept saying I was angry, but no one ever asked me why. They treated the symptoms but ignored the root. And I didn't know how to tell them what I couldn't even name for myself.

That same jail had once held my father. I remembered the illustrations he had sent, not to me, but to my brothers. Years later my oldest brother gave them to me. They were folded, worn, and sacred. I would use them in the children's book I wrote, pairing my words with his hand-drawn art. In a way, it felt like I was the author and he was the illustrator. Two broken stories told together, somehow redeeming both.

Years later, that same brother was in a motorcycle accident. My son was facing a health crisis at the time, and I felt like I was drowning. My brother suffered a traumatic brain injury. I stood by his hospital bed, and it looked just like the photo of our father in a coma. I realized: He's following those same footsteps.

He lived. He got a second chance. And maybe in that moment, I did too.

What I didn't know then, but would later find out, is that when he heard about my son's health crisis, he did something he'd never really done before. In his fragile state, unsure of everything, he turned to his wife and prayed out loud:

"God, if it's between me and that boy... choose me."

That prayer broke something open in me. A new level of forgiveness, grace, healing, and connection. It meant more than words could ever say.

Then, one day, he came to me. A TBI survivor who had been struggling deeply, mentally, emotionally, and physically, stood before me and said:

"I just needed to tell you... you are one of the strongest people I know. And I'm so sorry. Because this past year has been the hardest of my entire life. Needing help and having no one to help you, I finally understand how you've felt your entire life. And I'm so sorry."

It was one of the most healing moments of my life.

He was the biggest brother, the tough one, the one who caused the most chaos in my life and somehow, it was like he had been turned inside out. His emotions were on the outside now, raw and exposed, no longer tucked away beneath his hardened exterior. It was a version of him I had never really seen before. And in that moment, I saw more than just his pain, I saw his heart.

We had switched places. He saw me now. Really saw me.

At that time in my life, most people only saw the outside: the businesses, the charity, the giving. They didn't know I was in the deepest part of my healing journey. I was giving everything, my time, my talent, and my treasure, because it was all I had to give. I was trusting God with the rest.

I was part of the PTA then. At that time, I felt a deep calling to share my story about the impact teachers had on my life. When the opportunity arose to speak at an event, I believed wholeheartedly, This is my moment.

However, it didn't unfold the way I imagined. Instead of being given a stage, I was gently redirected to share privately during the teachers' morning prayer. At first, it hurt, I felt overlooked, misunderstood, even dismissed.

But as I stood quietly in the back of the room, I realized something powerful: my calling didn't depend on a microphone or a spotlight. My purpose wasn't diminished because it looked different from what I had pictured. God's plan was bigger than my own.

My husband later described it as walking through "the lions' den." And maybe it was. But standing there, silently strong, trusting God's direction rather than my own expectations, became one of the most defining moments of surrender in my journey.

I didn't need someone to hand me a mic.

God was building a platform I didn't have to ask for.

That day marked the end of an era. That community. Those friendships. Even the family circle.

God said, It's time to go.

And we did.

We put our house up for sale and within three days, it sold for $125,000 more than we bought it for. We packed up scared, unsure of the next step, and hit the road as a family of six for a full year. It was the most freeing, beautiful season of our life.

From hell... to honey.

God has always been there. Even when I didn't see Him.

That inner growth was happening long before it ever showed on the outside.

"I know the rules. Now tell me the fine."
—John Maxwell

Chapter Reflection:

7. From Hell to Honey

When did you realize something sweet was coming from your suffering? What "honey" has God given you after your hardest battles?

Let's Pray Together:

God, thank You for bringing sweetness from my sorrow. I never imagined beauty could come from my pain. Help me to see the honey in the healing. Let me never forget how far I've come. I trust You to redeem every hard thing for good.

Where the Story Begins

BEGINS, BEGINS, WHERE THE STORY
BEGINS....
ITS NOT THE MIDDLE OR THE END.

ITS NOT THE WINS OR THE LOSES,
ITS NOT THE WHAT OR THE WHO'SES.

ITS NOT THE TRIUMPH OR THE TRIALS,
ITS NOT THE RED CARPET DOWN THE
AISLES.

IT'S THE DOOR THAT OPENS AND YOU
STEP RIGHT IN.

ITS THE **LIVING** WHEN YOU SIMPLY JUST
BEGIN.

"

"THERE'S
ALWAYS AN
ALTERNATIVE
ROUTE."

Chapter 8: Pain You Couldn't See

"Becoming THAT Dreamer"

They say the path to success is a lonely one and whoever "they" are, they're right. But I never realized just how lonely it would be. I guess I thought that because I was chasing my dreams, overcoming everything I had for a reason that felt so important and so good, everyone would support me. That friends would join me, cheer me on, and family would be proud. That because I was doing it, they'd believe they could do it too.

I'd read about people who chased dreams and inspired others to do the same. But I didn't read the fine print, the part that said there would be sacrifice, loss, and pain, and that I'd have to overcome it all continuously just to get to where I wanted to go.

I think I thought that if God gave me the dream, then I would surely get there. But God gives you the dream, yes, He just doesn't tell you the path you'll have to take. And if He had, I probably would have stopped walking a long time ago.

People told me to just leave the past in the past and move on. That was so frustrating. I had left it, over and over again. But it wouldn't leave me. They said I needed to forgive and move on. I prayed endlessly:

"God, every time I remember, help me forgive again."

But I still had breakdowns. I still silently struggled. I had always known hyper-independence. I had always believed I was safer on my own. I had mastered the mask, smiling on the outside, dying on the inside. That felt like the story of my life.

I used to tell my counselor that I didn't even know how I really felt because I could mask it so well. But slowly, through her guidance, I started to learn. She helped me understand why I thought, acted, or responded in certain ways. She taught me to become aware, to recognize my patterns so I could take control of them and stop letting my past run my present and dictate my future.

Little by little, I chose to say, "No more." It wasn't easy. When your body has been wired to operate one way for thirty years, rewiring it is a battle. Healing for me wasn't pretty. It was raw. It was ugly.

No one tells you how painful healing is. How many times you cry alone while your body lets go of what it's carried for so long. How often you wonder if you'll ever be okay. If you'll ever actually heal.

I can't fully explain the weight of injustice I carried in my body. Or the confusion that lived rent-free in my brain. I had to untangle it all, piece by piece.

I had to learn to care for myself the way I always wished someone had. To be gentle, patient, and consistent. To tend to my pain, my triggers, my outbursts, not with shame, but with compassion. Every breakdown became a cry for love. Every step forward was a way of rocking myself through the nights no one else could see. And slowly, I began to grow.

The desert is one of the most barren places to be, but it's also where the most growth happens.

Healing made all the love songs feel like they were about me.

My dream. My life.

The enemy thought he stole it from me.

But now, it's my testimony.

That is the victory for me.

"There's always an alternative route."

Chapter Reflection:

8. Pain You Couldn't See

What pain have you carried silently? What would it look like to let that pain be seen and supported—starting with yourself?

Let's Pray Together:

Jesus, I give You the pain I've hidden. The hurt I've carried in silence. See me, love me, hold me there. Help me release the weight I was never meant to carry alone. Bring peace where there was chaos, and light where there was darkness.

66

"A PERSON
WALKING WITH
GOD CAN NEVER
GO IN THE
WRONG
DIRECTION."

Chapter 9: Your Turn—Becoming That Dreamer

"I Look to You"

A moment isn't a lifetime.

I needed a superhero, and I couldn't find her. So I became her instead.

In my children's book Little Lady, I wrote about how I once saw a beautiful woman, she was everything I dreamed of becoming. Beautiful and smart, talented, loving, and kind. Full of the fruit of the Spirit. And after a quarter of a lifetime, I finally found that the woman I was searching for… was me.

And I ended that book by saying:

"Why am I telling you this, you ask? Why is she important to you? Because little lady… that woman, she's you."

And that's true for you too, the woman holding this book.

You have everything you need to be everything you want to be.

There's a part of healing where you won't even recognize yourself, and that's okay. Resist the temptation to quit. Anytime you take a step toward the life of your dreams, anytime you take a risk or a chance on YOU, the first thing to meet you there is fear.

Nod. And keep walking.

Trust God. I once heard:

"No one said that trusting in God would take away your burdens, but it will make them lighter to carry."

That's the honest truth.

Listen, you take a hit in life one of two ways:

With your chin up, or your hands up.

Either way, you're going to get hit. Don't be afraid of the loneliness. It's where you find the aloneness with God.

Get clear about what you want. Write it down.

Feel excited about the thought of designing your life, and don't focus on what you don't have yet. Enjoy what you have while you work for what you want.

I got good at making things beautiful until I could have beautiful things.

Now I do both.

Get grounded in truth. Live a FitWithin life. Give yourself time. Be patient. Do the things for you that you once wished someone else would do.

Start treating yourself as the priority.

Romanticize your life. Wear the outfit now, not tomorrow. Do your hair.

Get dressed in a garment of praise every single day.

Designing a life you love is just that, design.

It starts inside and flows outward. Through your mind, your habits, your home.

Declutter.

And then declutter some more. Let go of things. Enjoy them in their time.

Be present. Let moments pass that need to pass.

Feel the feelings. Eat the ice cream. Use the cute cup. Journal. Draw. Create freely.

Make things nice. Do nice things.

Give yourself a chance.

Because you have everything you need to be everything you want to be.

Everything you've ever wanted is on the other side of an imaginary line.

Cross it.

This is a restoration of hope. A transformation in your life by the renewal of hope.

You are allowed to feel empowered to confidently take action on designing a life you love.

Because I know the value of a dream, when a dream is all you have.

Forgive the ones who hurt you. Forgive everyone, everything, and then forgive yourself.

Forgiveness is the key that unlocks the door to healing and walks you straight into freedom.

They did what they did. Things were how they were.

The story may have had a hard beginning but you get to write the rest.

The failures from them are opportunities for you.

God has a plan for you. Trust Him.

Job 23:14—"For He will complete what He appoints for me, and many such things are in His mind."

In order to live a life you love, you have to let go of living a life they approve of.

Stop facing reality. Start creating it.

You are an overcomer. Listen to what God says about you, not the world.

You are an overcomer.

And you too can be That Dreamer.

Let go of your past. Look toward your future.

Design a life you love—today.

And when you close this book, do something bold:

Write. It. All. Down.

Your goals. Your dreams. Your wants. Your wishes.

Have fun with it.

Then… start clearing. Start decluttering. Start transforming.

This is your catalyst.

Change your habits. Shift your thoughts. Break your addictions.

Reframe your identity.

Be a better woman, a better wife, a better mama, by giving yourself permission to become.

Let this book be your permission slip.

To forgive. To rise. To be happy. To start.

Because if you ask Google what it means to be a dreamer, it'll tell you this:

"Someone who spends a lot of time thinking about things they'd like to happen, but that are improbable or impractical."

Growing up, if someone said, "You're dreaming," they meant it wouldn't happen.

But being That Dreamer is different.

It's about a dream so big you have to tell the whole world to get just one person to listen.

I went from praying at Jesus' feet with my eyes shut... to standing up, smiling, and hugging Him.

That's what healing looks like. Not perfect. Not painless. But present. Bold. And surrendered.

That promise to never silence my story, no matter who's listening, became my vow.

And it still is.

The world won't understand your dream. That's okay.

Inconvenience means nothing when you're doing what God called you to do.

So don't give up.

This is your time.

YOU are THAT DREAMER

"A person walking with God can never go in the wrong direction."

Chapter Reflection:

9. Your Turn—Becoming That Dreamer

What are you dreaming for today? What does your next bold step look like in designing a life you love?

Let's Pray Together:

Father, I'm ready. Ready to dream again. Ready to design the life You created me to love. Walk with me into this new season. Remind me who I am. And when fear tries to speak louder than faith—whisper Your truth so clearly that I can't help but move.

Acknowledgments

"As long as you make sure that somebody else's life is OK, God will make sure that your life is OK."

— Inky Johnson

I believe this to be deeply true. Because without a few key people, my journey would still be one of struggle. I'd still be trying to figure it out on my own. Their presence and guidance were lifelines. Whether their impact was big or small, it was significant and their place in my heart is permanent.

It was as if the emptiness I carried from the uncontrollable parts of my past was slowly filled piece by piece, with their wisdom, kindness, time, belief in me, and their willingness to simply be there. These people are not just a part of my story. They helped rewrite it.

To Ms. Reshanna—thank you for fighting for me, for listening when I needed it most, and for never telling me who to be or how to feel.

To Steve—thank you for believing in my words and helping me find direction when I was lost.

To Jim and Carrie—thank you for not forgetting me. For believing in me when I couldn't see it in myself.

To Mr. Hall—thank you for standing up for those who can't always stand for themselves.

To the mighty entrepreneurs and everyday dreamers we've met along the way—thank you for showing up, standing tall, and inspiring others to keep going.

To my husband—thank you for not giving up. For being the steady anchor in my corner. Through it all.

To my children—thank you for loving me unconditionally. You are my arrows. My greatest joy. My biggest fans. I know without a doubt that God sent you to me.

To my mom - thank you. I love you.

And most of all…

To my Heavenly Father—thank You for never leaving me. Thank You for saving me. Thank You for giving me the strength to become.

References and Notes

Scripture References:
- Hebrews 6:19—"We have this hope as an anchor for the soul, firm and secure. It enters the inner sanctuary behind the curtain."
- Ecclesiastes 3:11—"He has made everything beautiful in its time."
- Hebrews 11:1—"Now faith is the substance of things hoped for, the evidence of things not seen."
- Job 23:14—"For He will complete what He appoints for me, and many such things are in His mind."

Quoted Individuals:
- Inky Johnson—"As long as you make sure that somebody else's life is OK, God will make sure that your life is OK."
- John Maxwell—"I know the rules, now tell me the fine."
- Deion Sanders—"Set your own thermostat."

Phrases Referenced in the Book:
- "It's not a tragedy, it's a masterpiece."
- "He thought he stole it from me, now it's become my testimony."
- "Writing my own treatment plan."
- "There's always an alternative route."
- "A person walking with God can never go in the wrong direction."
- "I look to You and not the left or the right."

Books Referenced:
- The Road Less Traveled by M. Scott Peck

Chapter Reflections:

1. The Girl with the Dream

What dreams did you carry as a child that still whisper to your heart today? Have you silenced them or are they still speaking?

2. The Turning Point—When the Dream Began to Pull Through

Can you identify a moment in your life when everything began to shift? What was God revealing to you about yourself in that season?

3. In Spite Of—Becoming Who I Was Always Meant to Be

What have you overcome that could've destroyed you but didn't? Who are you becoming because of that?

4. The Knock at the Door

What unexpected moment challenged everything you thought you were ready for? Did you rise or retreat? What did you learn?

5. More Than a Childhood

How has your childhood shaped the way you see yourself today? What are you working to unlearn or reframe?

6. The Road Less Traveled

What part of your healing journey feels the most lonely? What keeps you walking, even when the path is unclear?

7. From Hell to Honey

When did you realize something sweet was coming from your suffering? What "honey" has God given you after your hardest battles?

8. Pain You Couldn't See

What pain have you carried silently? What would it look like to let that pain be seen and supported—starting with yourself?

9. Your Turn—Becoming That Dreamer

What are you dreaming for today? What does your next bold step look like in designing a life you love?

Chapter Prayers:

1. The Girl with the Dream

God, help me remember the dreams You placed in my heart before the world told me to shrink. Remind me of who I was before I learned to doubt myself. Awaken wonder in me again, and give me the courage to believe that I was made for more.

2. The Turning Point—When the Dream Began to Pull Through

Lord, thank You for the moments that shift everything. Even when I didn't understand the pain, You were pulling me forward. Help me to see Your hand in the turning points of my story, and give me peace in the process.

3. In Spite Of—Becoming Who I Was Always Meant to Be

God, You saw me through every dark place I've walked. In spite of what I've been through, You are still writing beauty into my story. Help me shed shame and stand tall in who You say I am. Give me boldness to become all I was meant to be.

4. The Knock at the Door

Father, when life comes crashing in, help me not to fear. Even when I feel unprepared, remind me You are already in the room. Help me open the door with faith, knowing You go before me. Let me trust You when the unexpected comes.

5. More Than a Childhood

God, I give You the parts of my story I didn't choose. Heal the child in me who needed more love, more safety, more joy. Teach me how to parent myself with gentleness and grace. Thank You for giving me the chance to break generational cycles.

6. The Road Less Traveled

Lord, this road is hard, but I know You walk it with me. Give me strength when I feel alone. Remind me why I started, and help me trust that every step is shaping me for something greater. Keep me steady when I feel like turning back.

7. From Hell to Honey

God, thank You for bringing sweetness from my sorrow. I never imagined beauty could come from my pain. Help me to see the honey in the healing. Let me never forget how far I've come. I trust You to redeem every hard thing for good.

8. Pain You Couldn't See

Jesus, I give You the pain I've hidden. The hurt I've carried in silence. See me, love me, hold me there. Help me release the weight I was never meant to carry alone. Bring peace where there was chaos, and light where there was darkness.

9. Your Turn—Becoming That Dreamer

Father, I'm ready. Ready to dream again. Ready to design the life You created me to love. Walk with me into this new season. Remind me who I am. And when fear tries to speak louder than faith— whisper Your truth so clearly that I can't help but move.

About the Author

Elissa Stacy is a homeschooling mom of five, a faith-filled entrepreneur, children's book author, speaker, and founder of FITWITHIN and Tees for Truth. After years of breaking generational cycles and healing from childhood trauma, she now helps women design lives they love, from the inside out.

She's passionate about real conversations, raw healing, and reminding others that you don't have to wait to feel ready to begin again. Through her story, she hopes to be the flashlight for those still walking in the dark.

When she's not writing or creating, you'll find her homeschooling her kids, sipping espresso, or dreaming up her next big idea.

www.ingramcontent.com/pod-product-compliance
Lightning Source LLC
Chambersburg PA
CBHW051244120626
46547CB00014B/1793